Lessons I Learned As An Author

Sheldon D. Newton

Endorsements

This book is AMAZING. It is practical, thought-provoking and loaded with insight and information you need in order to become a successful author. This is a "CALL TO ACTION," which will motivate and inspire you to reach for your goal of being a best-selling author. Some books are all theory with no simple roadmap on how to get it done. This book by Sheldon D. Newton will show you how! He has done you a favor and written out a step by step exactly what you need to do to make it happen. I recommend this timely and fabulous resource to all who desire to write books that are life changing. If you want to know HOW to publish effectively and market your message to the world, I know Sheldon's book is right for you. So do yourself a favor, get this book and apply what you read. And see you on the bestsellers list.

Pam Perry, PR Coach, http://www.pamperrypr.com

The book "Lessons I Learned As An Author" is a very practical step-by-step guide on how to get started as a writer and follow through to the publishing of your work, and beyond that – tips for marketing the finished product. This book can save you tons of time involving researching the "how-to's" of becoming an author and publisher and also contains some awesome tips of the pitfalls to avoid in the process! Highly recommend it!

Deborah Moore
Author, One Thing Is Needful

This book is an excellent tool for the first time writer or even experienced writers. It is full of helpful information, instruction and insight that will leave the reader with answers they can use to write, produce and market their works. One of the most potent examples of this is the recognition by Mr. Newton that you are the one who has to drive your book sales, because your book listed on major sites does not mean automatic sales. Read and it is my belief that you will find many other insightful thoughts to help you on your publishing journey.

Dr. Dave Burrows – Author & Publisher
President & CEO One Rib Publications

YOU MUST HAVE THIS BOOK IN YOUR LIBRARY!!!

Written from personal experience, this book is just the tool you need to walk in the fulfillment of completing your book. I certainly wish I had it when I first started writing. Best Selling author Sheldon D. Newton has put together this gem, a masterpiece that will guide you and give you just the push you need to complete your assignment. I've always said that he is one of my favorite writers. This book further proves that.

Bestselling author Val Newton Knowles
Author of "Everyday Uplifting You," And "No Shame,
Only Power."
www.valnewtonknowles.com

Cover Design by Ashley Elliott Designs

Sheldon D. Newton
P. O. Box N. 10257
Nassau, Bahamas
Email: sheldond.newton@gmail.com

A JCCMI Production

Acknowledgement

I would like to thank Ashley Elliott once again for such a beautiful cover.

<u>Dedication</u>

I would like dedicate this volume to all of you soon to be authors who desire to write books and make an impact upon the lives of others for the better. May you rise up and become that author who helps to change the world in a positive way.

I would also like to express a heart-felt appreciation to those wonderful Book Coaches who have helped and mentored me along the way. They are listed in this volume along with their email addresses in case you would like for them to assist you as well. Believe me when I say that it would be worth it.

Pam Perry: www.pamperrypr.com

Rick Frishman: www.rickfrishman.com

Elder Paula Harper: www.wnlbooktours.com

John Kremer: www.bookmarket.com

LaTanya Boyd: www.latboyd.com

Dr. David Burrows: www.oneribpublishing.com

Contents

Foreword

"Lessons I Learned As An Author," by Bestselling Author Sheldon Newton, is a timely resource for any writer, teacher or aspiring author. Sheldon has done a remarkable job of sharing personal experiences, along with outlining a most comprehensive guide and blue-print on 'how-to,' get started in the literary world.

So honored to be Sheldon's Book Publicist and watch him take his writing career to greater levels. This book is indeed chock-full of resources, tips, and information on how to build a successful literary career.

Sheldon gives you the inside scoop – he's candid about what works (and what doesn't!) From how he ultimately decides what to write about, the research phase and the writing/publishing process of his books.

I'd scribbled down a page of notes, and had at least three big **'A-HA! Moments'** where I could identify things I'd been doing incorrectly or inefficiently. The most prominent message to me amongst all is to overcome any fear. What could possibly be holding you back from creating and completing a literary work of art? Stop procrastinating and bring your dreams to fruition!

–Lá Tanyha Boyd
Empowerment Coach, 3x's Bestselling Author & Book Publicist

Preface

I love writing. And I love being an author.

I first started writing over twenty years ago and to this day I am still thrilled when I am inspired to write another manuscript. And I also get excited when that manuscript becomes a book. As a budding author I experienced many things, some good and some bad. I learned about the publishing process and how it works. And I learned the difference between traditional publishing and self-publishing.

I also learned about co-publishing which is based upon a fixed agreement between the author and the publishing company. There are some things which I experienced during this time that, while I consider all of it as "learning" I would not wish to ever experience again. And I would do my best to help others avoid the pitfalls which can frustrate, discourage and even anger a beginning author. This is the reason for this book.

You represent the authors who may change the world by your poetry, biographies, messages, stories, thoughts and inspirations. **Please know this:** you have what it takes to write a good and ground-breaking book. Your book can make a difference. And you will leave this place armed with the wisdom and knowledge you need to make this happen. So, let me be the first to say, **"CONGRATULATIONS AUTHORS."** You have taken the first and necessary step. You are here. We will show you where to go next and what to do next. Get ready to learn, to apply and to experience success. This is your moment. This is your time. This is your adventure. *Sheldon D. Newton*

Chapter One
Do You Have A Passion For Writing

To date, I have written over ten books.

When people hear that, they look amazed and wonder how I was able to accomplish such a feat. I am a family man, a pastor, work at times as a Sales Executive for a leading Newspaper Company, travel to teach the Bible and still find time to write. "How," one may ask? The answer is simple. When something means something to you, when it is important to you, when you are passionate and feel strongly within about it, you will make time for it.

I love writing. I started writing when I was a teenager. Of course I wrote in school, doing class work, and at home doing homework. But when I became a teenager, I started writing using a yellow note pad. (I still do at times by the way). I wrote based upon what I was doing at the moment, which for me was studying the Holy Bible, God's Word.

As I read from Matthew through Revelation, I would write down things I came to understand. As a matter of fact, as I began writing things would just start flowing. I would write page after page from one passage of Scripture. The more I read the more I wrote. It was exhilarating. It was thrilling. It was exciting.

As time went on, I began to date a wonderful and beautiful young lady, who has since become my wife. I wrote her a booklet on my plans for the future, I mean in detail. She still has it after twenty three years of marriage, and at times reminds me of what I promised her I would do for her. (Maybe I shouldn't have written it down for now I cannot deny that I said it.)

Then came the time when I decided to write my first book. Now let me be honest with you when I say that writing a book, while to me is exciting, has also proven to be work. Indeed I have had to develop the habit of thinking things through and stating things in the clearest manner possible so that the reader can comprehend what I mean by what I write in the context that I wrote it.

I wrote a book dealing with the importance of unity. I ensured that I had my reference points and that I knew my subject. And this brings me to my first point about writing which is, **"Ensure that you know what you are writing about."**

Do not just write a book to write a book. I know that many people are doing that these days. But if you determine to be a real writer, I mean someone who speaks through the pen (or the computer), ensure that you write something of quality, something which can make a difference and have an impact upon the lives of those who may read it. This point is a vital key.

Action Steps: TAKE ACTION NOW

1. Determine your area of expertise. What are you writing about? **Who are you writing to?**

2. You will make time for whatever is vitally important to you. How strong is your desire to write and publish your book? Is it just a passing fad or is it a real desire? How big is your **"WANT TO?"**

3. Are you prepared to commit to working on your book? Commitment is not a feeling. It is a resolve. It is the determination that you will do what it takes to get to where you need to go regardless of how things appear or how you may feel. You will need to be committed to see your dream of becoming a best-selling author of books that make a positive impact on society become a reality. Are you ready to make such a commitment? If you are then you are half way there. A firm decision is a major key to getting where you desire to go.

Chapter Two
Get Past Your Fear Of Failure

Although I have written many books, I am amazed at how much there is to learn in regards to writing and publishing.

As I foresaid, the first lesson one should learn is to know what you are writing about. Know your subject. I cannot stress this enough. This will enable you to know your target audience. You have to know who you are writing to and for. There are literally billions of people on planet earth with all kinds of needs, desires, situations, circumstances and relationships. Your writing should be to address one or more of these needs or desires. This is vital for three key reasons;

1. When you know your subject you will give people substance. Your writings will contain value and quality. People will receive some wisdom, some answer that they are looking for. They may receive some entertainment value, filled with principles which can make their lives better. Write on purpose. Write to impact lives for the better even if it is fiction.

2. When you know your subject it will keep you focused. You will be able to stay on course with what you are writing about. This is important for it will ensure that your writing has structure and stability. You won't go all over the place.

3. When you know your subject it will give your writing credibility. When people realize that you know what you are speaking about and that they can therefore trust your words, it will enable you to stand out as an authority in the field you are writing about. It is not a good thing at all to have a book about a particular subject, with information which can be shot down easily because it is not built on truth or has very little, if any, factual substance (that is of course, unless your book is fiction). So make sure you have done your homework and write from a standpoint of knowledge.

The next lesson I remember having to learn is vital if you are going to succeed as an author. You must, **"Learn to get past your fear of failure."**

This was indeed a serious point for me. As I fore-mentioned, I wrote my first book, which was concerning the importance of unity. What I did not say then was that although this was my first book, I never released it. I finished writing it. And I even had a minister friend of mine do a foreword for it. But I never had it printed.

In retrospect, the book was really good (if I may humbly say so). It had substance and would have been a source of encouragement for many persons. But I did not have it printed. I wished that I still had it save on a jump-drive. I would surely have it published, at the least as an e-book. "Why didn't I get it printed," you may ask? The answer was that I was afraid. But of what was I afraid? I was afraid of several things;

1. I was afraid that people may not buy the book.

This fear was not warranted however. After all, I had no way of knowing if people would or would not buy the book. I cannot choose for people. People ought to be given the right to make up their own minds as to what books they should or should not buy. My job was to write it, get it printed or published, and then present it to them. But I did not do this because I allowed fear to stop me from moving forward. My question to you is, "Are you allowing fear to stop you from moving forward regarding your book?" If you are, it is time to get past yourself and to get past that fear. Some people may not buy your book. But, if you ask nicely, some people will.

2. I was also afraid that people would criticize my book if they read it.

I was scared that they would not find it interesting. And granted, some people may have negative things to say in regards to what you write. However, if you have followed step one, making sure you have written something of substance, worth and value, there will be others who will benefit greatly from your work. When I finally started getting my books out there it is amazing how many people told me the impact they have had upon them. This has transpired from my first book, *Diligence to The Things of God,* (available here: **www.sheldondnewton.org**). And it continues. Of course I have had some criticisms. But I have had more encouragement from the testimonies of those who found my books helpful. You never know whose life you can touch in a positive and powerful way. So step up to the plate, push past that fear and get your book written and out there.

In the next chapter I will share with you a third kind of fear that I experienced as I aspired to be a writer and it will be something of great interest to all who read this. I can promise you that it may be the number one reason why many have never even finished writing their book. I believe sharing my experiences with you may inspire you to rise up and realize your dream of being a published author, making a difference in the lives of others.

Action Steps: TAKE ACTION NOW

1. Ask yourself why you have not begun writing your book yet, finished your book yet or published your book yet? **Are you afraid of something?** What is it? Are you willing to push past your fear and do it anyway?

2. Realize you can write your book and publish it regardless of those feelings of fear. Do not listen to those feelings. **Write your book anyway.** Publish it anyway. "But suppose nobody wants to read my book," you may ask? Granted, some people may not. But mark my word: Some will. You will never know if you never try. So make up your mind to try and get your book done.

Chapter Three
Conquer Procrastination

I got my driver's license when I about thirty or thirty one years old. Now I could have gotten it before I turned twenty. "Why did I wait so long," you ask? The answer is simply because I procrastinated. Yes, I procrastinated, and for years. Now you may ask, "But why did you procrastinate, and for so long?" The answer is, "I was afraid."

Of what was I afraid? I was afraid of failure. I was scared of not being able to pass the Diver's Exam. I had never taken the test before. But I was afraid to try. So I prayed and asked God to help me get my license. Yes, I prayed. And I prayed for literally over ten years, asking God to help me get my license, refusing to do my part and take the test.

What was indeed interesting was that someone had spoken with one of my pastors, letting her know they were thinking of getting me a car. She told them that I did not have a license. So they did not give me a car. Then a friend of mine told me that she and her husband had a car for sale. They agreed to sell it to me for fifteen hundred dollars. I brought it. But because I did not have a license, I could not even drive it home. You should have seen me, the owner of the car, with my brother in law, me in the passenger side of the car, while he was in the driver's seat. He brought my car home for me because I did not have a license. As I would leave for work in the mornings, I would look over at my car and say, "I will drive you soon." Then I would go and catch the bus to work. When I came home in the evening, at times I would drive the car around in the yard because I was told to do this so that the car's battery won't die. As time went by, someone offered to purchase the car and for the same price that I brought it. I sold it.

What you may find interesting is that I brought another car. Yes I did. And I had my brother in law to drive it to my home for me once again, with me in the passenger side. Why? Because I did not have a license. Now, why did I not have a license again? Because I was afraid. Of what was I afraid? I was afraid of failure. You see, here in my country when taking our Driver's License Exam, we are required to be able to take a vehicle and place it between some plastic cones that are close together. Now it is possible to get the vehicle in the spot between the cones and get the vehicle back out. But many people had failed the test, and so I was afraid to even try.

After many years of praying asking God for my license, I believe God simply got tired of my stupidity. It dawned upon me that God did not have my license. The government has it. And it was up to me to go to them to get it. I thought "But I will have to take a test. And then revelation came, "Well, go and take the test" Again, I thought, "But I am afraid I will hit the cones (the inanimate plastic cones). And the revelation came to simply get someone to show me how to get in the cones. In other words, get a driving instructor. Finally, after over ten years, I stopped procrastinating and did something about my situation. I got a driving instructor to show me how to do it. She immediately saw that I could drive. I told her where my concern was and she took me out by the cones and showed me how to get in and out. After about three sessions, she put in for me to take my exam. And I passed the first time. Many people don't, but I did.

Now I could have been driving for years. I could have driven my own car. But I kept putting off what I could have done and should have done in order to get my license. I was praying when I should have simply taken a few steps and gotten my license.

Now while this story may be amusing for you, consider this; Are you procrastinating in your writing because you fear that people may not want to read what you have to say? Are you afraid of failure so you make every excuse as to why you cannot finish what you have started?

If you truly want to write you will have to learn to **"CONQUER PROCRASTINATION"** and get your book done. This is the valuable lesson I wish to leave with you today. Learn to conquer your fears. You know what you want to do. You know what you need to do. Now master and conquer procrastination, and get it done. You will be glad you did.

Action Steps: TAKE ACTION NOW

1. Do you feel strongly about what you are writing? Your passion is what will push you to complete your book.

2. **Focus on your objectives.** Think of the advantages of being a published author. Think of how many people you can inspire, entertain or even perhaps help. Think of the monetary rewards it can offer to you, your family and others you desire to assist, but lack the resources to do so. Ask yourself if the rewards of being an author outweigh your fear of failure. I can guarantee that it does.

3. Stop putting off writing or finishing your book. Get to it. Make it a point for the next thirty days to work on your book, even if you only write small amounts. **Work on it DAILY.** A word of caution here: Do not neglect your family or your responsibilities. But for thirty days do your best to push your book as far as you can **DAILY.**

Chapter Four
Pay Attention To Detail

One of the greatest lessons I learned as an author is the importance of **paying attention to details** when it comes to properly preparing your manuscript.

I well remember when I was in the process of publishing one of my books, and I believe one of my most unique. I had acquired the services of a particular company who also provided editorial services. The lady that was presented as my editor, upon editing my manuscript, sent it back to me for review. I noticed that despite my best efforts on my own, I had quite a few mistakes. The editor made some corrections, but I saw more that needing fixing. So, I pointed them out and resent the manuscript back to the editor.

She made further corrections and resent the manuscript back to me, and again I pointed out some more that needed correcting. After about three times back and forth she proceeded to say the following to me; "Sheldon, regardless of how many times we correct a book, there are always minor errors in them."

She was saying this to me so that I could move ahead with publishing. Now, at that time, in order to be a peace-maker, I said, "Okay," and the book went on in the printing process after making a few more corrections. But it was a mistake to do so for there an error of the same word in varied forms at least three times in the book, which may have been caught if we had paid attention to details.

I had paid for the services of this company, and while it may be true that regardless of how many times a book may be edited mistakes are inevitable, the truth of the matter is that efforts should be made to ensure that they are kept at a minimal or eradicated all together. It is possible.

The editor should have never said what she did to me. She was only attempting to hurry me along in the printing process. I paid for this service. She should have been willing to do what it takes to ensure we presented our best to the public.

After the book was printed, a friend of mine, and fellow minister contacted me regarding the errors which I had in the book. The word that desperately needed correcting was totally inaccurate in its settings. Since then I have taken the book from that particular company and personally corrected those errors.

This experience, along with a few others, taught me a valuable lesson, well actually, two lessons. **Number one; "When I am paying for a service, speak up for myself."**

Whatever company I am paying is not doing me a favor. They are being paid to render a service and I have a right to demand their best. **The second thing I learned was that it is vitally important, even though it can be tedious at times, to re-read the manuscript, even after receiving editing, until I am convinced that it is ready, before I let the printing process continue.**

I would greatly encourage you to do the same. **Pay attention to detail.** Go over and over your manuscript. Do spell checks. Ask someone who is good with the English language or whatever language you are writing your book in, to go over your work for you. If they offer advice which may make your book more readable and effective, receive it. Be open to learn. Hire the services of a professional editor if necessary. This may again be tedious for a real editor may work you. But believe me when I say it will pay off in the long run.

Action Steps: TAKE ACTION NOW

1. **Always do spell checks on your writing.** Ensure that your writing is clear and understandable for your readers. When you write a chapter, or you may prefer to wait until you have finished the manuscript, do spell checks even before you send your work to an editor.

2. If you have a close friend or relative who is good with reading and spelling you may ask for them to critique the manuscript for you. They may give you some wise counsel. If they do, **TAKE IT.**

3. Find an able and competent editor to edit your work for you when you have done all you can do yourself. This is a must. There is nothing worse than trying to read a book filled with grammatical errors which should have been corrected before going to print. By the way, it has been my experience, that regardless of how many times I personally go through the manuscript myself I still miss grammatical mistakes. So I have learned to let an editor re-check my work because I have found it is an absolute necessity.

Chapter Five
Know Your Subject

What are you writing about? It is vitally important that you write what you know about.

Granted that if you are writing fiction you are free to use your imagination. But if you are writing non-fiction you need to do your utmost to ensure that you are writing from a solid foundation of truth and experience. Your motive for writing must have an objective, a positive one, one that can add or even multiply worth and value to those who read your book.

I know that many people are writing books these days, and that is fine. But it is a noteworthy fact that people who know **why** they are writing, and who have **a focus** and goal to impact the lives of others end up going places. You should not just write a book to say that you have a book.

What are you writing about? To whom is your message intended? When people read your book what do you want them to receive from it? How will it better their lives, their situations and circumstances? Write with purpose.

Each of my books are written for very specific purposes. For instance, *"Diligence to the Things of God"* is written to help people see the importance of reading their Bibles and daily prayer. It also instructs on the importance of forgiveness and how to actually do it. So many people are in bondage to their emotions in this regard. They want to forgive, but do not know how to do so. Principles I share in this book, both from the Bible and my own experiences shows the reader exactly how to forgive, why they should forgive, and how to walk the process out until their feelings come in line.

My book, *"My Name is Jealous,"* shows readers how to develop a more closer and ever-increasing intimacy with God, which will then filter down into all of the other areas of our lives. People are sharing with me how that book has changed their lives. Its purpose is to encourage the reader to deepen his or her walk with God.

Now my book, *"How To Live The Christian Life Successfully,"* is geared towards teaching people how to live victoriously for Christ on a daily basis. It is actually a handbook on how to live for God day by day. Many have shared with me how that particular book is really changing their lives. What I would like you to see is that each of my books has a purpose. Each carries a message, a central theme, which can propel the reader into a greater dimension and level of living.

While it is an awesome thing to be a published author, it much greater to be an author whose work has a positive impact upon society.

So you must examine the reason why you desire to write a book and ask if you have something worth sharing. I believe that each of us has something to offer. All of us have been given talents and abilities from God with which we can impact people's lives for good if we will focus and develop those giftings. As it pertains to writing books, I believe that anyone who aspires to write one can do so in such a way that it has positive impact, provided that the writer does his or her homework and ensures what is written is done so from the foundation of knowledge, wisdom and experience which makes our words credible and transforming.

As it pertains to this particular book you are reading, my objective is to share with you what it takes to be a writer of substance, one who can, through the art of writing, help others live a successful, victorious and over-coming life. I love seeing people handle their circumstances and situations in a manner that will produce wholesome change and bring glory to God.

God has a plan for each of us and it is my burning desire to help people discover their purpose and walk in it victoriously. This burning desire is what is behind the messages I teach, the seminars I hold and the books I write. **What motivates you?**

I encourage you fellow writer to make a firm decision that you will write books which can help, uplift, encourage, motivate and inspire others to live a better quality of life and make a difference in the world. These kinds of books will endure for years to come.

Action Steps: TAKE ACTION NOW

1. It is vitally important that you know what you are writing about. So carefully define your subject and your objective. In other words, do you even know what you are talking about? Do you have experience along the lines you are writing about? Suppose you are asked to come and give a lecture along the lines of your book. Can you do so? Is your subject a part of you?

2. What impact do you want your book to have upon your audience? Again, knowing what you are writing about and who you are writing to will help you to answer this question. You will be remembered for your impact upon society. So will it be positive or negative? It's up to you.

3. Even if you write fiction ensure that your book has a central message, a positive message so that it can leave a pleasant note in the soul of the reader. Do not just write foolishness. Someone may believe you, follow your seeming advice and do something stupid.

Chapter Six
Think Things Through

It is sad, but nonetheless true that while there are over seven billion people on the face of planet earth, **there are not a lot of thinkers.** Most people just accept whatever society says without using the mind God gave them to think things through.

The art of thinking has been lost at great peril to mankind, for most people think of thinking as too much work. Why think for ourselves when we can just go with the flow and receive whatever comes to us through the various mediums of television, radio, music, and the like? However, true thinkers are deeply concerned with the state of the world because it is headed to destruction at a very fast rate of speed and the seeming "powers that be" have no idea how to control or stop it.

While I am not trying to be a party-pooper, I must let you know that I refuse to let society tell me how to think. In an age when wrong is being called right and right is being called wrong, I purpose in my heart to stand with God and with the Bible regardless of how old-fashioned people may desire to label me.

Why am I speaking like this in a book that is geared towards teaching those who desire to be writers how to hone their craft? The answer is because if you are to amount to anything as an author you will have to learn to be a thinker. You will have to rise above the noise and speak in your writing with an authority that stands out loud and clear.

Beyond this, you must learn to think your subject matter through. Do not write just because you have read someone's work and felt that you could write a similar book using different words. Some people do this. If your book is to be of substance you will have to learn to study and research your subject. Understand that thinking things through will aid you greatly in not being scattered in your thoughts. To write with unfocused thoughts will prove to make your writings seem confusing.

I know that some may disagree with my thought regarding this, but I will state it and allow you to come to your own conclusion concerning it. Writing a book of quality and substance is an art. It is the result of giving great thought and attention toward the subject matter until the essence of what you are writing literally consumes your thoughts and make an impression in your soul.

To write without considering the results of your thoughts may prove detrimental to your writing career if you do not ponder your steps carefully. I believe that when a message consumes us it may not even take a long time to write it down. I am speaking here from experience. I know what it is to write three books within a year, and each of those have proven to be a blessing, help and inspiration to those who have read them. Contents for books which can be a help to humanity flow through me constantly.

If I can give you some advice along this line I encourage you to weigh your subject matter carefully and write from your heart. Write in a manner that will be sober and clear-headed. Make sure that your writing is not here and there. Learn to keep your thoughts structured so that as you write the information will flow and you will not seem to be writing from the state of a confused soul.

This will prove helpful for you will want those who read your first book to look forward to reading whatever you put out next. If they find your writings full of substance with material which helps them and shows them how to enjoy a better life, they will want to read more from you, and perhaps even to hear you speak in person.

Do yourself a favor okay? **Do not think of how you can make money first. That will come as people find out you have something worthwhile to offer.** Think of how you can make a difference in a person's life sharing what you know. That is writing with quality and substance. And that is the kind of writer you should aspire to be.

Action Steps: TAKE ACTION NOW

1. This chapter was written to help you examine your motives for writing. The art of writing and impacting people's lives is of such an immense value that we should never take for granted people will believe what we write. Somebody will. They are looking answers and when we put a book out there on that particular subject, they will assume that we are the authority upon that subject. Someone may act on what we say. (What a serious thought.) Financial gain will be a part of what you receive from your writing efforts. But ensure that you are writing to help people, to make their lives better or to entertain their thoughts with something which will make their day brighter and perhaps their burdens lighter.

2. Write down your objectives regarding your book. When people read your book, what do you want to happen in their hearts and minds? What impact do you desire to make? What message do you want them to take with them when they finish your book? Knowing and keeping these things in mind will help you stay focus as you write. Your thoughts will seem more together.

Chapter Seven
Write Down Your Thoughts

As you think upon the subject you desire to write about you will find thoughts coming to you constantly, and perhaps even when you are not expecting them. **Write those thoughts down before you forget them.**

It has been my experience that when inspiration comes, if it is not grabbed and written down quickly, it may be lost. I received insight into something which I neglected to write down right away and I forgot it. I have never, even up to this day, gotten that insight again in the manner that I did on the spur on the moment. This has been some years ago.

I may have gotten a similar thought, but the way the inspiration came was so good. I just wish I had written it down when I first received it. This taught me a valuable lesson. Now when inspiration comes to me of something which can help me or others I write it down.

I usually attempt to keep a pen and something to write on around me. But I also use the writing pad on my phone to make notes. I encourage you to do the same.

Inspiration can come at any time, and seemingly from anywhere. It is vital that as it comes, we as writers and authors write them down so that we can ponder them. Please do not leave it to your memory to recall that flash of truth which can come at any moment. I really believe that these precious gems which come to us are from deep within, in our hearts. This is why we may not recall them after they are gone.

Someone has said, **"Pen to paper never forgets."** I agree.

Here are three reasons you should always keep something handy to write down flashes of inspiration as they come:

1. **You won't forget them.**

2. **You won't let them get away from you.**

3. **You will be able to go back to your notes and see how wonderfully what you have written fits with what you are writing.**

This is a word of advice that I surely hope you would heed. It will prove to be to your benefit and the benefit of those who read your book.

Action Steps: TAKE ACTION NOW

Make it a point to write down those inspirational thoughts which can be placed in your book when they come.

DON'T MISS THOSE MOMENTS.

Chapter Eight
Be Open To Change

A teachable spirit will always excel because a person who is always open to learn will always advance in life.

If you are going to excel as an author you will have to learn to listen to others who may know more than you. Criticism is not always a bad thing. And while most of us do not like being corrected, it is true that correction of a positive sort always proves beneficial.

When it comes to writing I have had to listen to my friends and editors who gave me great advice in regard to my manuscripts. Sometimes I may not necessarily have liked what was said, but putting aside my feelings and really listening to what was being said helped me hone my writing skills and avoid unnecessary embarrassment.

For example, I once had a book cover produced which simply put, did not look good. A friend of mine, upon seeing it, told me never to put out something like that again. Although I may have felt a little annoyed at his honesty, I must admit that he was right. The cover simply did not look good. As a matter of fact, I acquired the services of a Book Coach to promote this particular book. After she found out I was about to release another book, she asked if we could center the Book Promotion around the newer book.

Later, when I was telling her what my friend said about the cover of the former book, she said, "I don't like it either." This was apparently why she preferred to do the promotion around another new book instead. Another friend of mine did not like the cover and said that a seven year old could do a better job. Of course, my wife did not like it from the beginning. I should have listened to her. Now, I had to be willing to look objectively at what people were saying in relation to the cover. And I had to be willing to accept constructive criticism without getting offended.

You may ask, "What did you think about the cover?" My answer would be that it could have been done much better. My wife was right, my friends were right, and it did me good to hear their opinions in this regard.

If you are encouraged by professional or well-meaning people to have your book professionally edited, do yourself a favor and listen to them. It will prove to be great advice when people comment on how well your book is put together.

If they advise you to change some things around in your book, look at what they are saying and see if doing so will make your book better and more effective in the lives of those who read it. **Encourage feed-back** even before you publish your book from people you trust who can offer their wisdom in this regard. It can save you a lot of time and money if you do this right.

Chapter Nine
After The Writing

After writing over ten books I can attest to the feelings we experience when we know we are done. However, permit me to caution you in this regard.

Writing the book and getting it edited is good. But now we will have to consider several other things if our books are to go out and bless the world, and in return, prove to be a blessing to us as well. Writing the book is not all there is to it. You will have to think about getting the book from a written manuscript to becoming an actual book.

This is where I will have to open up about some issues and experiences I have had along these lines. I remember after I had written four books that I felt the need to go to a Book Conference in Los Angeles and hear some experts in this field share with those of us who desired to be successful authors. I had four books out, but was not attaining the level of success I wanted and needed in this arena.

I believe that some of the greatest and most effective authors of our time were there in that room, willing and eager to share with those of us who attended. Some of them said some things which I learned from. And I was really impressed by a few of them. But there was one who really got down to it and spoke directly to my situation in a clear and dramatic way. I will tell you why I say this.

I had assumed some things that were not accurate. And I believe that most of us are presuming the same thing. I thought that writing the book and then presenting it to a traditional publisher was all I needed to do. I was wrong, dead wrong. I found out real quickly that regardless of how well a book is written, and how good the author thinks the book is, as a rule, traditional publishers do not take first time authors, unless you are willing to purchase a huge amount of the books yourself.

My first book was rejected by a major publishing house who said it was not what they were looking for at the moment. So my first, second and third book were self-published. You may ask, **"Is self-publishing worth it."** That depends. I will however address that issue in another chapter. But permit me quickly to point out that many who have self-published their books have had tremendous success as an author, and some even became best-selling authors. Their books have done well and they have even made great sums of money from the sales of their writings. There are even those who have suggested that after what they know now, they will not let a traditional publisher publish their books anymore. I personally believe that there is benefit in both, depending on what you do and depending on what you are able to persuade the traditional publishing house to do.

But permit me to get back to my point and my story. I had become very frustrated after bringing out four books and seeing little returns. This was why I went to Los Angeles from the Bahamas to attend this particular book conference. It was worth every bit of what I spent to get there and more. Even though many of the speakers were saying things here and there that may have had somewhat of an impact this one speaker in particular brought it home for me. In his presentation he said something along these lines, "Let me tell you what some of you are thinking. You are thinking that you are going to write a book, send it to a traditional publisher and just sit back and watch the money roll in." **Who told him?** That was exactly what I thought. And because it did not happen that way I was disillusioned, discouraged and discontented. I was upset with book companies. And I needed someone to set me straight and show me how this business really operated.

Then the speaker said, "That is not how this business operates. Your book is just that, **"YOUR BOOK."** And if it is going to sell, "YOU" are going to have to make it happen."

WOW. That was an **'AH-A Moment'** for me. It was a **'ALLELUIA Moment.'** It was an **'EYE-OPENING Moment'** in deed. This was actually what I needed to hear. And I heard it.

It was not the responsibility of the book companies to make my book take wings and fly. This was **NOT** their book. This is **MY** book. And I was going to have to assume responsibility for it. This was a life-changing moment for me as an author. And I hope it will prove enlightening for you too.

Stop depending on the book companies to make your book a success. Most of the time, and I do mean ninety to ninety eight percent of the time, you will have to show the traditional book companies that your book is worth investing in by selling several thousand copies of your books before they even look your way or invest their money in helping you to push it. I am sharing this with you hoping to help you steer away from being confused and frustrated like I was. I can sense that some of you are have an **'AH-A, ALLELUIA, EYE-OPENING MOMENT'** like I did.

Please remember this, **"YOUR BOOK IS JUST THAT, "YOUR BOOK." IT, THEREFORE, WILL BE YOUR RESPONSIBILITY TO PUSH IT UNTIL IT TAKES WINGS.**

Chapter Ten
Traditional Or Self-publishing

Now that we understand our book is our book and that we need to take some responsibility for what happens to our book, let me speak of the importance of selecting the right book company to publish your work.

We will have to address the subject here of **Traditional publishing and Self-publishing.** Please understand that I am not comparing the two. That is not my purpose here. As I intimated in the previous chapter, I believe there is merit in both, depending on the author.

But again, it is a noted fact that most of the manuscripts presented to a traditional publisher are rejected if the person presenting the manuscript is not already a famous personality of some sort. If you are someone of renown who has thousands and even better millions of people who look up to you and love what you have to say, I believe traditional book companies would probably tear down the doors for the opportunity to represent you and even present you with a large advance for your book.

But if you are like I was, a seemingly unknown, your book will have to be out-standing, I mean brilliant, for them to even consider publishing it. And even if it is an excellent work most of the time it will be rejected. Traditional book companies do not want to give advances and place money behind a project that has yet to prove itself. Most of the time they need a guarantee that your book will sell, and that guarantee is you proving that it is sell-able by selling several thousand copies.

So most of us will have to self-publish first and prove our 'weight in sales' before traditional companies want to speak with us about an advance royalty paying contract. But take heart for while this may not seem fair, it may prove to be the motivation we need to take action, sharing with others why they should invest in what we have to say. Do not see this as a negative thing. Instead, consider it an opportunity.

Self-publishing is not all bad, or as in my case, it is not bad at all. Actually, it is quite adventurous. Here are just a few of the reasons why you should embrace this opportunity:

1. **With most self-publishing companies you have total control.** I know that some people may say that you have control with all of them, but that has not been my experience. Some self-publishing companies can prove to be quite pushy. But seeing that you are coming up with the money to pay for the services you desire do not let them push you around. If you do not like a cover they design, send them back to work. If you do not like the format and lay-out of the book, ask them to change it. Be forth-right and objective in your answers. If you are paying, get the service you desire and expect excellence from the company you choose. There are so many self-publishing companies around right now that you can pick, choose, refuse and even fire. I had to do just that to at least two of them.

2. **If you choose a good self-publishing company, you can get much better royalty payments for your books.** I have some things to say along this

line in another chapter, but permit me to speak a moment from my heart and my years of experience as an author of over ten books. In my personal opinion some self-publishing companies are nothing but con-artists operations. They do not have the author at heart. They charge huge amounts of money for services which they may not even render. This has proven to be a source of great discouragement for me. And after these years of learning how some of them operate, I can let you know with assurance that there is one thing I will never, ever do again. Never again will I pay a self-publishing, non-advancing company huge amounts of money to publish my books. I am not speaking here of paying for copies of the book. I am speaking of paying great amounts of money to simply get the book formatted and published as a book. Paying for the copies is a different thing altogether. Hear me and hear me well; If a book company wants to publish your book and wants you to pay thousands for doing so, (again, I am not speaking of getting copies of your book. I am speaking of the publishing process of designing, and formatting and getting your manuscript ready for printing), I strongly encourage you to not go this route. I will address this further later. But I do hope you heed my wisdom in this matter.

3. If you have friends like I do, or people who have publish their books before, and you can get a proper edit of your manuscript, or perhaps a great cover designed or maybe someone to format the inside of your book for you, your book can look great and you can avoid paying for some of the special services which self-publishing companies offer. I would advise that if you need to have the book professionally edited and you do not know

an editor, please use the service provided by the book company. Your book must be edited properly so people can enjoy it when they read it. People like me do not like a lot of typos when we read. I allow a very good friend of mine, who is also an author and an editor, to edit my books. She has done better work with editing my books than some companies I paid for the services. (That's just the honest truth. She is very good at what she does. She found errors and typos in my books that other editors missed.) So she edits all of my manuscripts. Then I have two dear friends of mine who are excellent when it comes to graphic designs. They create my cover designs and even create the cover itself. (I know. God is good to me.) If you have people in your life that can help with these things then you may not need to pay for these services. A word of caution here though: Please ensure that the person doing the editing or your book covers are professionals and know what they are doing. Covers sell books. So your cover must stand out. And the book must be edited and typeset properly.

4. **When you self-publish you retain all of your rights to your book.** Therefore, if you sell a good amount and get the attention of a traditional publisher, who offers you a good advance and a great deal, you are able to take your book from the self-publisher with no side effects and drama. They will release you. I really like the idea that I retained my rights to my books.

These are just some of the advantages of self-publishing. There are more. Please note again that you can become a best-selling author even though you are self-published. This has been proven time and time again. I have done it. And so have others.

If you can retain the services of an agent, who has the ear of a traditional book publisher, and can get you a great deal, go for it. To get a great advance from a traditional publisher for your book is a goal you should set for yourself. But most of the time the traditional publisher would not take you book unless you can prove its sell-ability, as I foresaid. So set a goal to sell five to ten thousand copies of your book and then a traditional publisher may be happy to speak with you about taking the project over.

What I wanted to stress is that even if your book is rejected you do have options and the ability to bring out a quality book which can impact the world. So do not allow yourself to be discouraged. Self-publish if you must and then push your book remembering that it is just that, **"YOUR BOOK."**

Action Steps: TAKE ACTION NOW

1. Your book is your book. And it is your responsibility to push and make it go. This is where **GOAL-SETTING** is an excellent ideal. Begin to set a goal of selling a certain amount of your book each week or month. One thing that is great about self-publishing is that you can order any amount of copies you want, from one to one thousand. So if you can only afford fifty or one hundred and sell them and then get some more, **DO THAT.** But whatever you do, set a goal as to how many you want to sell within a year and **WORK TOWARDS THAT DAILY.**

2. Understand that some self-publishing book companies can help you to market your book if you pay for their services. Get all the help you can. But do not just depend on them. Learn to sell your books yourself. Prepare your mind for this now even while you are still writing your book.

Chapter Eleven
Make A Good Appearance

A good book cover can sell books.

My sister works in the hotel industry here in the Bahamas. At the time of this incident she worked in the Accounts Department of a very prestigious hotel. She had taken some copies of one of my books, *"Humility and the Honor of God,"* with her to work to help me sell them. One of her supervisors saw the book and said, **"Appearance is everything."** The cover was so beautiful and out-standing that he purchased a copy even though he apparently did not embrace Christianity.

So your cover matters. Make sure that you get a graphic artist to create a state of the art cover which can cause people to take notice. Your cover should be a calling card that summons those who see it. It should say, "If you like me on the outside imagine what you will find when you read me."

As I said previously, some of my covers were not good. They did not speak to people who saw them. They did not say, **"Pick me up and read me."** Some of this was my fault. I am about to offer you some advice which may prove very helpful as you pursue a publisher for your book. Do yourself a favor and be up-front with the publishing company, especially with the graphic artist. This is doubly true if you are self-publishing your book.

I was once afraid to tell the publisher what I really thought of the cover design because I feared hurting their feelings and because I just wanted to hurry and get the book done. My friend, let me say that if you are paying to get the book done, do not be afraid to tell the publishing house what you do like and what you do not like as it pertains to the cover of your book. If you believe a better job can be done, do not settle for less.

My cover on one book was simply not attractive at all. So, seeing that it was self-published, I took it from that publisher and re-published it with a much more suitable cover design. If I had been up-front with the publisher from the beginning I may not have had to do that. So I am not blaming that book company. I signed off on it even when I had reservations within.

Amidst the fact that I write because I love and have a passion for it, I had to come to a starling realization which I trust that you understand as quickly as possible. Once you have written your book and placed it in the hands of a publisher you are now a business person. That's right, you are a business owner. You have a title. Your title is, **"AUTHOR."** You have a company, **"A BOOK COMPANY."** Yes, I know we have various reasons we desire to publish our books, but in the final analysis we must see that we now have intellectual property which we must manage well to the best of our ability.

Some people write and produce books primary for the money. That is their focus and aim, to make money and lots of it. Others write for the fame and popularity it may give them. Still others write to leave a memoir of their lives for their generations to come. Some write to share with others how they got where they got or how they became successful in their business endeavors. And some people write to inspire others, to motivate and challenge them to reach out and be all they can be, to seize their destiny and make something of themselves.

Some write to share education of various sorts with the world. They produce educational literature which people can use to excel in their schooling. And some, like me, write to share spiritual realities with people enabling them to grow and develop in the relationship with God. There are other reasons why people may write a book as well. Some people simply desire to share their thoughts and feelings with others. Writing is how they expressed themselves.

It really fascinates me how fiction writers can put a novel together with all of its intricate ideas and thought-provoking sequences of events that you can hardly wait to turn the page to see what will happen next.

I have a friend whose mind works like that. It seems as if a novelist mind sees in pictures in such vividness and clarity that it is like a movie, a motion picture taking place. When they speak to you based on their thoughts they create an image within your mind which makes you see what they are seeing. This is the gifting of a true story teller. As they share they pull you into their world.

Again, regardless of your reason for writing, you must embrace the fact that when you become an author you now own intellectual property and you are now in business. Make sure that your product goes to the public looking good. Ensure that the cover stands out. **Even if it does not look extravagant, it should look elegant.** So do not settle for anything less.

Action Step: TAKE ACTION NOW

Find someone who can create you a book cover that rocks. You will need this to attract attention to your book. You can find them on the internet by doing a search. Or you may have a friend (like me) who can help you. Or then again, the book company you choose to publish your work may offer you a good cover design as a part of their package. But whatever you do get a good cover done.

Chapter Twelve
Some Facts In Regard To Self-Publishing

Most of my books are self-published. And I have learned some very interesting things along my journey thus far as an author.

Some self-publishing companies are very good and very good at what they do and provide. They really try to help authors have a grand experience and work diligently to help writers realize their dreams of becoming an author, then pushing and inspiring us to do what we can to make our books best-sellers. So I speak reluctantly when I say that not all of my experiences with self-publishing companies were pleasurable.

I will not point out any particular company. Instead, I would simply like to offer some advice and hope to steer you in the right direction as you pursue your goals. I know what it is to pay too much money for my books to be published. I know what it is to pay little. And I know what it is to pay nothing. **(That's right, I said, nothing.)** This applies if you know how to format your own manuscript, get your own editor, and get your cover designed on your own and ready for print).

In my humble opinion let me say here and now as I have said before, **"I will never again pay a lot of money to get my book self-published."** I don't care what they claim to offer. The truth is, as you will see in the chapter regarding **MARKETING YOUR OWN BOOK,** you are going to have to learn how to **MARKET YOUR OWN BOOK, PUSH IT AND MAKE IT GO.**

Some self-publishers will say that they will market your book by placing it on amazon.com or on Barnes & Noble's website, and many of them do this. But if you think that your book will sell just because it is on one these sites you are sadly mistaken.

When I first got my book published I thought that because it was on these sites and available to distributors, my book was going to just take off and sell. I was wrong.

But this was not the thing which made me wary of some self-publishing companies, for they did what they said they would do. They did make the book available on **Amazon** and **Barnes & Nobles.** What up-set me was when they promised what all they would do and how they would put out a television commercial to over one hundred thousand people, when it seems evident that they did not do this.

If you think I am venting, I am not. I am simply hoping to help you see that you cannot pay attention to all of the seeming fluff that some companies try to put out there, all in an attempt to get your money, and afterwards move on to their next victim, not really aiding you and assisting you like they said they would. Actually, all they kept doing afterwards was try to get me to purchase more and more copies of my books from them.

Actually, when I share with you what is expected of you if you are going to succeed as an author, you will realize that you should not be expecting the self-publishing companies to spend much time pushing your book. You will see that it is your responsibility to show people why they should get your book and the value it will add to their lives.

So my aim here is not to point out flaws of self-publishing companies. Rather, it is my feeble attempt to share with you the importance of being able to discern the good from the not so good. Most self-publishing companies basically say the same thing and basically offer the same thing. There are exceptions to this rule, but for the most part they really offer the same. However, some of them charge large amounts to offer you what you can get for little or no money. Make a firm decision to look at all of the pros and cons of the companies which interest you.

Read all of the details and then do a search on the internet concerning that company and others. Compare them. And if possible, check their work. You can look at books they have already done on Amazon or elsewhere. Here are just a few tips:

1. There are many ways to self-publish and many self-publishing companies. Do your homework and check them out carefully. See what they offer. Make sure that you choose one which also places your books on Amazon, the largest search engine on the internet.

2. Do not choose a publisher that is charging you large sums of money just to publish your book. Granted that you will have to pay for copies of your book which can prove to be expensive depending on how many books you order, it is simply not necessary to spend huge amounts of money to get your book done.

3. If the Book Company is editing your book, when they send it back for you to read over, read it over. Do not just say, "It's good to go." Pay attention to detail and make sure that all of the things, as much as possible, that needed to be

corrected have been corrected. Do not be in too much of a hurry that you bring the book out with a lot of unneeded and un-necessary mistakes. If you find that more corrections are needed ensure that they are done. You will be glad that you did. Don't let that company rush you. You are paying for their services.

4. If the book company is doing your book cover, ensure that you choose one that is elegant and beautiful. **Your cover is a big part of your marketing plan.** Sometimes if people are attracted to the cover they may buy the book. This has been proven in my case.

5. If you have someone who can an edit your book properly and someone who can format your book, and then someone who can provide you with a beautiful cover, you may be able be able to get your book done for little or nothing. When I say nothing, I am referring to the fact that CreateSpace.com offers you the opportunity to get your book done **FREE** once you have already edited your book and can get the help to format your book and design a professional cover. **(If you need help with this I have placed the names and email address of the professionals I use at the end of the book.)** Then again, there are other companies which will do your book for you for just a few hundred dollars. When companies start asking for a few thousand, it has become my pattern to stay clear of them now. This is just me after being burned somewhat through the years. It is simply not worth it. Not a one of the companies which charged me over one thousand dollars for their work has proven that they deserve another opportunity. Not one.

It is my desire to help you avoid the disappointment, frustration and anxiety I have experienced. If you have the money and you want to go that route that is up to you.

Chapter Thirteen
Some Myths About Marketing Your Book

I shared with you in another chapter how I attended a Book Conference in Los Angeles in which one of the speakers said these words, "Some of you think that you are going to write your book, present it to a publisher and then you are going to sit back and just watch the money roll in. That is not how this works. Your book is just that, **YOUR BOOK. AND IF IT IS GOING TO GO, YOU ARE GOING TO HAVE TO MAKE IT GO.**"

This bit of advice made a world of difference to me. Actually, it was like a breath of fresh air. It took away much of my frustration with various book companies and showed me that it would be up to me as to whether my books sold or not. Sure, the book companies may have a part to play. But in the final analysis if it is to be it would be up to me to develop a strategic marketing plan and get the news out there about my books and the impact they could have upon the reader.

What is marketing? It is helping people to see why they need what you have to say. It is showing them how what you say in your writings will impact their lives for the better. **Real Book Marketing** is actually showing people how your book will add or even multiply value to their lives. Here are a few things Book Marketing is **NOT;**

1. **Book Marketing is not just placing your books or having them placed on Amazon hoping that people see them and buy them.** Positioning your

book in the right places like Amazon or Barnes & Nobles etc., is vital in your book marketing efforts, but you must realize that over one hundred thousand books are published each year. You must be able to show people why they should choose your book over the hundreds or thousands in your genre.

2. **Book Marketing is not waiting and hoping something happens.** If your books are going to sell you will have to be a willing participant in the process. Like me, you may have to hire a publicist to help you learn how to share with the world with you have to offer. If you need to, get one. There are many of them who are very good at what they do and also very affordable. Some that I have worked with include, **Ms. LaTanya Boyd, Mrs. Pam Perry, Mr. Rick Frishman, Mr. John Kremer and Elder Paula Harper.** (Their contacts are at the front and back of the book.) Hey, if you approach any of them to help you with your marketing, please let them know that you learned about them through my book. They may give you some extra help. They have all been very kind to me.

3. **Book Marketing is not bombarding people with your book on Social Media Sites.** Yes, you can share about your books and writings on the various sites and you should, but you do not want people to feel like you are just a 'Sales Person' trying to make a buck. You don't want to come across that way. If you need to, get some training on how to interact with people so that they will see you as someone desiring to add value to their lives rather than someone just trying to sell a book. As a Sales Person in a leading Newspaper Company in the Bahamas I can attest that

relationships matter. And if you can establish good relationships with people on the social media sites it will make a world of difference. They will support you. They will want to support you. And they will even tell their friends and those in their circles about you. Getting others to vouch for you will prove to be an amazing booster to your marketing efforts. So shoot for developing relationships and showing people how much you care about them. It will be a tremendous help in showing them why they should purchase a copy of your book.

4. **Book Marketing is not being idle, waiting for your cheques.** Make up your mind that you will learn all you can about how to market your books. **Apply what you learn. Keep at it. Persevere. Never give up. Your efforts will pay off.**

Now that we have looked at what book marketing is not, let us see some practical tips to effective book marketing.

Action Steps: TAKE ACTION NOW

1. Start researching ways you can market your book. You can watch some videos on Youtube.com with authors who have been successful at marketing their books to learn some keys to effective marketing.

2. Begin making a list of things you can do to market your book, showing people how it may impact their lives in a positive way.

3. Aim to be creative in your Book Marketing Goals. Think outside of the box.

4. Ensure you get a coach who can help you get out there. Some are listed in this book at the back.

Chapter Fourteen
Good Advice From A Leading Author

Some time ago, after I had written about four books I wrote a best-selling mega-star author, via email, to ask for some advice on how I could become a best-selling author.

This distinguished gentleman is still one of the leading authors in his field. As a matter of fact, he is one of the most out-standing authors in the world. I am both humbled and elated that he took the time to read my email and then to send me a personal letter through the mail with encouragement, inspiration and advice. From that moment to this I have remembered three pieces of instructions he gave me and I would like to share them with you. (I know you may want to know who I am speaking of, but in this case, you will have to trust me when I say that if you knew who he is, you would pay very special attention to what he had to say. Out of respect for him I will not call his name.)

The first thing he advised was really about what he and his partner did when they released their first book. They sought opportunities to get on the radio talk shows and share about their book as much as possible. They made it their determined focus and business to do at least five things daily to advertise and push their book. They literally went on all of the shows that would have them. This worked greatly in their favor. He encouraged me to do the same.

So this is the first piece of advice I would like to share with you. **Embrace every form of media, radio, television, newspaper, magazines (both print and on the internet), as much as you possibly can.** Ask radio hosts if they would allow you to come and share with their audiences. They are always looking for people they can have on their program. Why not you? Make yourself available. You may say, "I'm afraid to go on radio." Well, the good thing about the radio is that nobody is seeing you. So they will not see that you are nervous. (Don't tell them, okay?) Just go on the show and share your message from your heart. Another word of advice here is, **"Do not be so concerned about telling people about your book and where they can get it when you are on the radio. Instead, share your message. Let the audience feel as though you are attempting to help them, provide answers to their questions and solutions to their problems. Let them sense that it is your desire to help them be better, do better, live better. Let them see you care. When the time is right, the host will ask you to let them know about your book and where it can be found. Your focus is to be adding worth and value to people's lives. The rest will take care of itself."**

Take as many publicity opportunities as you can. The more you do, the more people will get to know who you are and hear your message or read your message. (By the way, having a good Book Coach can help to get you radio and magazine publicity. Some good ones are listed in the back of this book. So make sure you get their addresses and write them. They will prove to be an asset to you in your book marketing endeavors.)

The second word of advice to come from this mega-best-selling author really stayed with me as I hope it will with you. He said in his letter to me, **"Market your book strongly for at least a year."** This advice shows the depth of value he placed on the importance of marketing.

It is vital to the success of any book. **So promote your work. Share it with others. Push and get out there.** Do not be afraid to let people see what you are about and how you have something to say which can make a difference in their lives. Go on the internet and learn from others how they got publicity opportunities. Provide press releases to the media which caters to the people you are attempting to reach. Do not wait on the book company to do this for you. **Do what you can.** And like the out-standing author said, **"Market your book strongly for at least a year."**

The third bit of advice that this **author** shared with me was, **"NEVER STOP MARKETING."**

This shows the power of persistence. Market your book strongly for at least a year. But what do you do after that year? **NEVER STOP MARKETING.** You may need to remember this when discouragement comes and tries to park on your shoulder. May you hear that still small voice within encouraging you to keep on keeping on.

There is something about being consistent and persistent that causes things to work in your favor after a while. It seems like **SUDDENLY** things which you wondered if they would ever happen, happens, and in such big ways that it blows your mind. Listen, you can be a best-selling author. You can sell lots of books and make a huge difference in the lives of others. You can share your writings, wisdom, experience and ideas with the world. **BELIEVE.**

Believe enough to keep on keeping on. Believe enough to reach out. Believe enough to push and help as many people as you possibly can. It will be worth it.

Action Step: TAKE ACTION NOW

1. Have you started making a list of how you will market your book yet? If not, **GET TO IT.**

2. Make a list of family and friends you can approach, asking for them to support you and purchase a copy of your book. Try to get your list to one hundred persons or more. Add to it as you remember more and more people or meet more and more people. And don't forget to ask your co-workers. Some will say no. **BUT SOME WILL BE PROUD OF YOU AND SAY YES.**

Chapter Fifteen
A Publicist Can Help

I shared with you in a previous chapter how I got various publicists through the years to help me with marketing my books. Their advice and coaching still continues to prove immeasurable and advantageous to me.

If you are a writer, but lack skills when it comes to marketing your books, I would advise you to seek the help of these willing and able professionals who can help you with developing your platform and establishing your brand. They will also set you up with various radio interviews and may even help you do what is termed a **Blog Tour.** It was after I asked for help that I became a best-selling author. You have to know where your limitations lie. I know that some people may have a problem with that statement in this age when we are told that we can do anything. The truth of the matter is that we all need help at some time or another.

It is good to know where your strengths and weaknesses are. If you know you need help marketing, ask for it. If you are financially able and can delegate this service to others, it may be to your advantage. When I accepted the help of the publicists which helped and continue to help me, I did not have much money. So I choose those who I could afford. And to me this was best, for they did not do the marketing for me. Instead, they taught me how to do it for myself. Seeing that I am constantly writing and producing new books, I am glad to know I can use these same marketing techniques to market all of my writings. **AWESOME.** This chapter is really short, but it also offers some of the best advice I can offer you. And that is, **"IF YOU NEED HELP, GET SOME HELP."**

Action Steps: TAKE ACTION NOW

1. Do you need help with your marketing? Do you need a Publicist? If you do, make contact with one of the ones I mention below. Or search online for another.

2. You need to arrange a Blog Tour for your book. Contact a Publicist and let them help you with this. Again some great ones are listed right below. I used their services. They are good.

3. Get some good marketing tips from Mr. John Kremer, author of the best-selling book, 1001 Ways To Market Your Book. He is really an author's friend. Find his site here: www.bookmarket.com

LaTanya Bloyd: www.latboyd.com

Mrs. Pam Perry: www.pamperrypr.com

Elder Paula Harper: www.wnlbooktours.com

Rick Frishman: www.rickfrishman.com

Chapter Sixteen
Overcome Your Fears

When I brought out my first book, *Diligence to the Things of God,* I ordered a thousand copies thinking that I knew at least that many people or that many people knew me. I expected to have sold that many books in a short period of time, probably a few weeks or a couple of months.

Well, it did not work out that way. Despite the fact that I was a travelling minister of the Gospel and that I was well known in some places, I was amazed that not many people purchased my book. And believe it or not, after receiving some seeming rejection, I started allowing fear to stop me from asking people if they would like to purchase a copy. This is why I really attempted to encourage you in the first few chapters **NOT TO ALLOW FEAR TO STOP YOU.**

I know first-hand how it can paralyze a person.

I actually began giving away my books free, continually. Books I had paid for. Books I had paid thousands of dollars for. It was really foolish to do so, but I was ashamed to ask people to buy a copy.

I found out something else too. I remember asking a dear friend if she would like to purchase a copy of my book. Her response was not something I expected. She said, "You should give me a copy." She made me feel guilty for asking her to purchase a copy. That really got me. I had paid to get these books done. Why should I give them away free? And yet I did. So let me give you a bit of wisdom that I have learned. **When you publish your book and purchase your copies for resale, do not be ashamed or afraid to sell them.** Do not give them away. You may have a certain amount that you would like to invest in a few special people's lives. That's okay. But what I am attempting to emphasize is that if you are to succeed as an author you will have to refuse fear as if it is a plague. You will have to be bold and ask people to buy your book. You may ask, "But what if I ask someone if they would like to purchase a copy of my book and they say, "**NO?**" My answer to that is something I learned as a Sales Executive for the oldest Newspaper Company in the Bahamas. Simply say, "**NEXT.**"

Ask enough people and someone will respond positively. Do not take the 'no' to mean that your writing is no good or that people will not want to read what you have to say. **SOMEBODY, SOMEWHERE NEEDS WHAT YOU HAVE TO SAY."** Remember that.

Fear is an evil thing. It robs people of their potential, of their ability to rise up and seize their destiny. Fear will cause you to think that because one person says no, everyone will say no. **DO NOT BELIEVE FEAR. FEAR IS A LIAR.**

You have written your book. You went a step further and edited it to the best of your ability. Then you solicited the help of a professional to edit it. You went ahead and got it to a publisher and you paid for copies so you could share what you have with the world. **DO NOT LET FEAR HINDER YOU NOW OR STOP YOU FROM MAKING A DIFFERENCE IN THE LIVES OF THOSE WHO NEED TO HEAR YOU.** Even if you feel afraid, still ask people if they would like to support you by purchasing a copy of your book. Some will ask you what it is about. After speaking to them passionately about it they will tell you that they don't have any money at the moment, but they will get back to you. And they never may. Some will ask you to give them a copy free, and may attempt to make you feel guilty for not doing so because of your friendship or family relation.

Then again, some may tell you that you are not a writer and that you are wasting your time. But if you stay with it, there will be those who become so touched by your passion or simply by the fact that you have persevered and become an author that they will count it an honor to support your efforts.

I am a living witness that if you **stay with it and never give up, overcoming your fears and persisting in your efforts to better lives through the power of a book, your diligence will pay off and you will be glad you did not give up.**

You may ask, "But what do you do regarding those friends who insist that you should give them a copy because of your friendship?" My admonition is simply, "Follow your heart." If you had it in mind to bless them with a copy do so. If they ask for a copy and you know that they are without a job and cannot afford a book, and your heart is moved, go ahead, if you want to, and give them a signed copy. If that friend freely helped you with the project, using their expertise to help with editing or with a cover design or maybe even with suggestions as to how you could make the book better, then it may be proper to accommodate them with a gift copy of your work, and even with an acknowledgement of their help and your appreciation in the book.

However, remember that you paid to have your book published and paid for the copies. So ensure that you sell your work, bless, inspire, encourage and entertain others with your writings, and make a profit from your labor. Do not feel guilty for doing so either. And if someone is your true friend he or she should want to support you. If they can afford it and yet they are demanding that you give them a copy, then you need to see if that is the kind of friend you want in your life. I'm just saying.

.

Action Steps: TAKE ACTION NOW

Have you started making your list of family, friends and possibly co-workers whom you will approach concerning supporting you by purchasing a copy of your book when it is done. If not, **GET IT DONE NOW.** Remember, procrastination will hinder you from reaching your goals. The time to planning your marketing strategy is not after your book is done, but before.

Chapter Seventeen
Receive Help From Family And Friends

I shared with you in a previous chapter how going to a Book Conference in Los Angeles really change my perspective regarding my responsibilities as an author.

I had assumed that it was up to the book company who published my writing to make my book go and sell. So I was truly disappointed when it seemed as if the book company was not pushing my book. But, as I learned in this Book Conference, it was not up to the book company to push my book and make it a best-seller. It was up to me to create buzz for my book and show people how what I had to say would add worth and value to their lives.

This knowledge really was the **EYE-OPENER** that I needed. And I began to build my platform online. What do I mean by my platform? I am speaking of creating an online presence of yourself in the area you are gifted to help people. In other words, creating an online presence is showing and sharing with people online of your knowledge and wisdom. It is aiming to help people with what you know, developing relationships and impacting as many lives as possible with what you know.

There are many people who need answers to the various areas of their lives. Someone has said, "If you want to be successful help as many people as you can." I believe that this is why real success evades many. They are so busy trying to just get money, just trying to get people to purchase a book. You may have a measure of success there. But if you really want to make it big, try to see how many people you can help. It will make a world of difference in your approach to people and in their response to you.

One of the keys of effective book marketing that I have learned to take advantage of is allowing my family and friends to help me sell my books.

When I published my first book, I asked some of my family members to help me sell some of them. They did. Even my mother got involved.

Since then, I have continued to ask for help in selling my books. I have found that there are people who will help you if they can. Some may say, "I am not a Sales Person. I cannot take hearing no when I ask someone to buy your book." But again, as I said that I learned as a Sales Executive for a major Newspaper Company, just say, **"NEXT."**

Someone will help you. Someone wants to help you.

People know people. This is the reason you need to ask for help in selling your books. Your friends can reach their friends who can reach their friends and so on. I also learned to offer incentives. I would say to some, "The book is for $15.00. If you help me sell them, you can give me $10.00 and you can have $5.00 for each book that you sell." Some take advantage of this offer. Others will help me and give me all the funds, desiring to help me with no strings attached. I remember giving an entire box of twenty-four hand-back books to a member of our congregation to sell for me, offering her the same incentive. She brought me all of the money, refusing to take anything. God bless her for her kindness and consideration.

I once gave a friend a copy of my book, *My Name Is Jealous,* which is a devotional on developing a closer walk with God. She told me how that particular book really had a strong impact upon her. So much so that she refused to lend the book to anyone. She did not even allow her special friend or her sister to borrow it.

She would have brought a copy for them but I was sold out. (It is still one of my most selling books). Even after she finished the book she refused to lend it out. I am in the process of revising the book, including a section for questions and meditations. She wants a copy of that one too. I told her that I would give her one if she would agree to sell some for me. And she has agreed to do so. What I am trying to point out to you is that there is no one way to sell your books. Think outside of the box. Look for ways to get your work out there. And if family and friends are willing to help you, let them do so.

A word of caution here though; **Make sure that the friends and family you ask for help are trust-worthy.** Money has a funny way of not only bringing out the best in people, but also the worst. So be careful who you allow yourself to get into business with, okay.

Chapter Eighteen
Blog Blog Blog

I shared with you how I received help in marketing my books from several Publicists who taught me how to create an online presence. One of them said something to me that I have now learned is vital to engaging your target audience and building relationships.

Although it has been some years since she said it, it took me a while to understand the importance of it. She said, **"Never leave a blog site unattended."** I had started a blog site, **(sheldondnewton1.blogspot.com),** but was not using it daily, weekly or monthly. When my coach found out about that she said those words to me. I did not understand however how important it was to maintain a functional blog site.

Blogging is one of the main ways to continue to share your knowledge and wisdom with people who need what you have to say. It helps you to remain a part of your customers lives even after the book sale is completed. You can actually engage your audience by giving them the ability to respond to your blogs. If they like what you say they may share with people in their circles. That can increase the number of people who learn about you and what you have to offer by way of information and books.

I read and learn from professionals in the book marketing industry. And the one thing I keep hearing from them is about the importance of maintaining relationships with your readers through blogging. I strongly encourage you to get a blog site if you do not have one, and start engaging your audience.

You can use your social media sites to encourage people to check out your new blogs. Twitter,Facebook, LinkedIn etc are all avenues where you can engage your friends and customers and let them know that if they like what you are saying, they can find more information at your Blog Site.

If you are like me, you may help in learning how to set up a Blog Site. You can find people to help you online. As a matter of fact, you can go to Youtube and put in the words, **"How To Build A Blog Site)"** People will come up who will show you exactly what to do and how to do it. It is easy and you can have your site set up in a short while.

I am now blogging at various places every week. And it is yielding results. People are reading what I have to offer. Some are not responding favorably to my blogs. But most of the response is positive. I remember a former pastor of mine telling the congregation, **"Whenever you say something you are running the risk of being misunderstood."** So do not expect everyone to agree with you or like what you have to say.

If what you are saying is truth and if it can help people and add worth and value to their lives, then impact your world for good.

Action Steps: TAKE ACTION NOW

1. **Do you have a Blog Site**? If not, get one, or get a website on which you can post your writings. If you need help regarding this, a publicist can help. Or you can learn about it online. Do your research.

2. When you get your Blog Site, **BLOG, BLOG, BLOG.** As one of my coaches told me; "NEVER LEAVE A BLOGSITE UNATTENDED."

Chapter Nineteen
Learn To Follow Instructions

If you determine to get a publicist or coach to help you develop your platform and establish your online presence in the area of your expertise, then I have a word of encouragement and warning for you:

LEARN TO FOLLOW INSTRUCTIONS.

It is not the instruction given, but the instruction received and acted upon which yields results. For you to hire a coach as I have done, and refuse to carry out his or her advice is a waste of your money and their time.

It is vital that we all learn to do what we are told when it is on our own best interests to do so. However, some coaches will tell you that they have clients who simply will not become an active participant in their own success. They want the coach to do everything for them.

As real book coach will not allow you to make them do all the work. That is not their purpose. They have not been hired to market your books for you. Rather, their job is to teach you how to set yourself up for success as an author and how to market your books for yourself. I believe that a Coach's greatest joy is to see you so established as a professional in your field that you are selling hundreds of thousands of books and building more and more relationships.

I also believe that it is the aim of all good coaches to help you push your first book while teaching you how to do it yourself so that you will know how to sell every other book that you publish.

All of the coaches whose services I retained are very, very good at what they do. And I have lessons from them that I will continue to implement for all of my books as I continue to write. Each of them gave me instructions. And they fully expected their admonitions to be carried out. They even set deadlines of when they expected to follow up with me and make sure I was doing what they asked. One of my coaches even got on my case when that I was not sticking to my commitment to do as she instructed.

A coach will do actually what that term means. They will coach you. **DO NOT EXPECT A COACH TO MARKET YOUR BOOKS FOR YOU. THEIR JOB IS TO TEACH YOU HOW TO MARKET YOUR BOOKS. FOLLOW THEIR INSTRUCTIONS AND YOU WILL SEE RESULTS.**

If they set up Radio Interviews for you, show up and on time. Be there when the host ask for you. If you are asked to be a blog which will be hosted on other people's Blog Sites as a part of your Blog Tour, write that blog. Write it to the best of your ability. Write it in a timely manner. **DO NOT PROCRASTINATE AND WAIT FOR THE LAST MINUTE. GET IT DONE.**

Do your best not to frustrate your Book Coach. If they ask you to do something and you do not know how to do it, ask for their help right then. Do not wait until the appointed time. When the coach asks you if you completed your given assignment, your response should not be, "I didn't know how to do it."

If you don't know how, let him or her know before the due date that you need some help. That is what your coach is there for, to help you. I am grateful to my coaches all of whom I highly recommend.

If you need some coaching and some help in building your author platform, there are professionals who can help you. If you want to go on a Blog Tour which includes Radio Interviews and being able to place your writings, your blogs, on other people's sites, then these coaches and others are there to help you make it happen. Again, if you need help, ask for help. There is no shame in that. I have listed a few of them in the back, whose services I highly recommend. So please check them out.

By the way, if you have not yet set up your Author Central Page or your Blog Site or your own Website, these coaches may be able to help you get it done. I can vouch for them for I have used their services. They are here to help you. They want to help you. And they are well able to help you. So click onto their website, check them out and initiate contact with the one who offers what you are looking for. Say, let them know that Sheldon D. Newton recommended them.

Chapter Twenty
The Joys Of Being An Author

You may ask me, "What is your greatest joy as a writer and an author?" My answer will immediately be, "When someone shares with me how something I wrote helped them and changed their lives."

I was speaking with a lady who owns her own business. She has a hair salon. She proceeded to me how she had read one of my books four times and was on her fifth time going through. She was reading *My Name Is Jealous.*

She told me of how one of her workers asked her to use her book. She would not lend it to her. A customer wanted to borrow it. She would not let them use it either. The book had such a powerful and life-transforming effect upon her that she held it dear to her heart. She told me that she felt I had written that book just for her. It touched her deeply within.

Another lady who had purchased the same book told me that it was the best book, beside the Bible, she had ever read. And another told me of how much that book had impacted her life.

To me, knowing how my books are really giving people hope, help, inner healings and answers that they need is such a joy. It really makes a difference. This is why I encouraged you to make sure you become a writer of substance, someone who writes to impact people's lives in a good and positive way. To realize that something you say inspires somebody to make a change, or motivates a person to reach for their goals will prove to give you a sense of happiness on the inside that even money cannot buy.

Here is a question that you need to answer: What do you truly want to accomplish with your writings? I know that many of us may say, "I want to become a millionaire." But beyond money, what do you want your writings to do. What impact do you want your books to have upon people who read them?

I want to write to help people. I desire to share with people what I learn about living for God. To me there is no greater privilege that exists. And when people let me know of the impact my books have on them in this vein, it gives me joy.

So my bit of wisdom here is, find out why you want to write (beyond the money you would get from it) and purpose in your heart that you will make a difference in someone's life.

Action Steps: TAKE ACTION NOW

As an author, what would give you the greatest joy? Why are you writing? What is your objective? Knowing why you write will give you great passion for writing on purpose.

Chapter Twenty One
Final Words: Never Stop Marketing

Many people give up too quickly.

They quit when the going seems rough. They fold up because things don't look as if they are working out. But you should never stop marketing. You should be in this for the long haul. You should have a made up mind that you will write your book and finish what you started. And when you have finished publishing your book, get copies and begin selling them. Then get more and keep on keeping on.

Learn to market your books on the internet. Push and do your best to find out what others who are best-selling authors and who have already proven what works do and practice what you can. Keep on learning more and more how to share with you know.

Keep on engaging people on the Social Sites, making new friends and meeting new people. Keep on blogging. Never quit. The word that the mega-bestselling author rings out loud and strong: **"NEVER STOP MARKETING."**

As I end this particular book, I trust that you learned some things which helped and encouraged you in your writing endeavors. Here is a poem I wrote that I pray will stay with you and give you that added zeal to keep on keeping on until you get your book written, then published, and until you become a best-selling author, making a difference in the lives of many people.

Don't Quit
Written by: Sheldon D. Newton Sr.

The highest steps, the greatest dreams
Did not just appear by any means
But were the results of an inner quest
That passion that would not quit or rest
Until it found the thing desired
Would do whatever was required
A visionary with a steady heart
Would find some way to produce his art
That picture that is seen within
Even though without there's no resource to begin
Yet the dreamer still holds on
Knowing that it won't be too long
For if there is a dream there must be a place
A path, a plan, to run the race
Visions, they are meant to be fulfilled
Its secret lies in the power of will
The Will of God must surely be
For if not, why would He show me
All things are possible if I just believe
I can do This, I can achieve
Hear the dreamers of the past give a word
Don't quit

Don't give up when things don't seem to fall in place
Don't you dare give up and quit the race
Mountains in your way, a storm in your path
Don't you let them extinguish that flame in your heart
For the dream is bigger than the obstacles of life

They are only stepping-stones for one in the fight
You are the victor, for God lives within
His wisdom will show you how to win
Don't quit, don't give up, just keep pressing through
And you will succeed in that which you do
No matter how long it may seem
If you refuse to quit, you will realize the dream
Keep praying and reaching for all that's within
You are bound to come out on top, you will win
The vision is yet for an appointed time
To give up now would be a crime
For this dream that you have, this vision, this plan
Is not just for you, but for others, and
If you dare quit they may never see
All that they can really be
Hold on, stand strong and you will aspire
To that dream that you carry, stay on fire
Don't quit.

Remember Joseph over in Canaan's land
Received his dreams from the Almighty's Hand.
Scorned by his brothers, his father too
Could not see what Joseph knew
Hated, abused, and sold as a slave
Joseph held on to the vision God gave
There in Egypt, a free man bound
No love one there to help him now
And yet this dreamer pressed his way
He refused to waver, choose not to sway
With a focused mind he moved ahead
Even in the midst of so much dread
The dream within was greater still
When challenged, lied on and thrown in jail
Joseph continued to dream his dream
He would not let go by any means
And when the time was right this dreamers dream
Became a proven thing, yes it came
To pass. Because Joseph would not quit

God brought him through and he still had his wit
He is an example to you and I
To tell us, we can do it, be it, if we try
God's grace is all the strength that you need
You need not worry about defeat
For through Christ Jesus you are the victor, its true
He is willing and able; He is there to help you
Don't quit, your dreams fulfillment is just ahead
Just keep going, you'll be glad that you did.

Prayer of Salvation

God loves you and has provided the gift of salvation for you. This gift is in His Son, the Lord Jesus Christ.

To receive God's precious gift, you must receive Jesus Christ as your Lord and Savior. To do so simply pray these words and mean them with your whole heart:

Oh God in Heaven. I come to You in the Name of Your Son, the Lord Jesus Christ. I am a sinner. I need a Savior. Jesus is that Savior. I believe that Jesus Christ, Your Son, died for my sins. I believe that He was buried and that You raised Him from the dead. And right now, I receive Jesus Christ as my Lord and my Savior. And because Your Word says that if I do this I would be saved, I want to thank You right now for saving me and washing my sins away in His precious blood. In Jesus Name I pray, Amen.

According to the following passage of Scripture, if you do this, you can be assured that you are now a child of God.

Romans 10: 9
"That if thou shalt confess with thy mouth the Lord Jesus, and shalt believe in thine heart that God hath raised Him from the dead, thou shalt be saved."

If you enjoyed this book please check put these other books by Sheldon D. Newton

Genna's Fight (A Novel)

My Name is Jealous

How To Live The Christian Life Successfully

How To Pray & Get Results

The Powerful Ministry Of Intercession

Humility & The Honor of God

Diligence to the Call Of God

How To Hide God's Word In Your Heart

Thrown Away(A Novel)

If you enjoyed this book, kindly leave a review on amazon for me. It does not have to be long and I would really appreciate it. Thanks for sharing.

Sheldon D. Newton
P. O. Box. N. 10257
Nassau, Bahamas.
www.sheldondnewton.org

Email Sheldon D. Newton at:
sheldond.newton@gmail.com

A "Breath-taking" Novel that keeps you glued to every page

Read the fictional story of a lady who endured abuse and scorn from her child-hood and even through her marriage. Watch as she is literally kicked out of her home and forced to leave her only son behind. Will Genna survive? Will she overcome? Or will she commit suicide?

LEARN HOW TO WIN IN LIFE!!!!!

DILIGENCE

The Master Key To Achieving Your Dreams

Reaching Your Life's Goals With Focus, Determination and Faith

Bestselling Author Sheldon D. Newton

Your goals are truly possible if you believe enough to pursue them relentlessly.

Learn How to Pray Effectively for Others

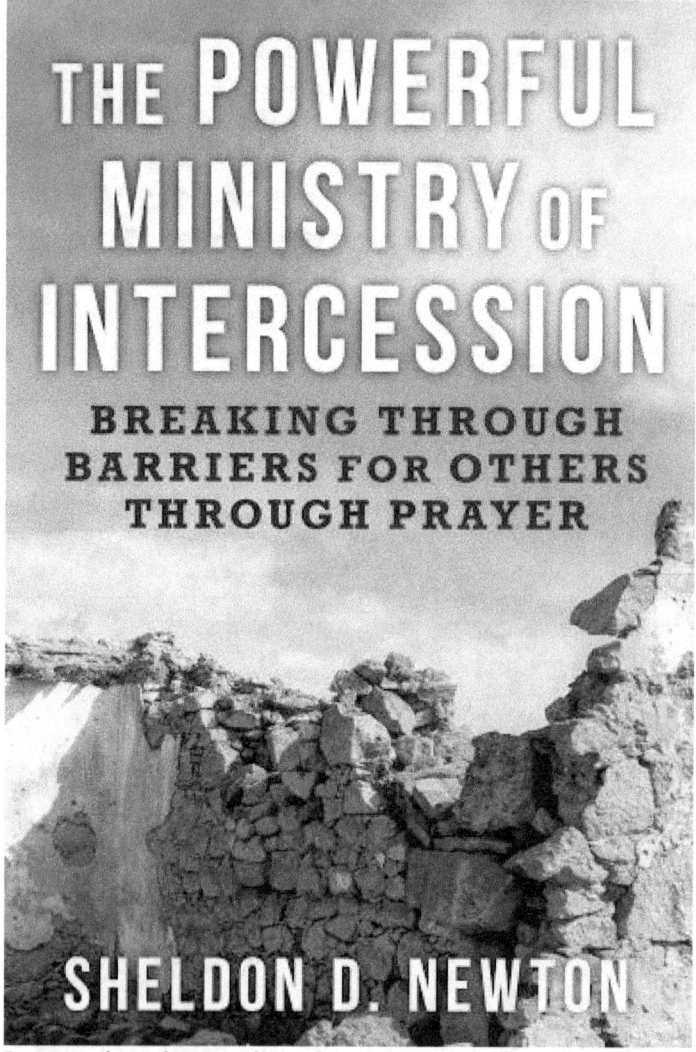

THE POWERFUL MINISTRY OF INTERCESSION

BREAKING THROUGH BARRIERS FOR OTHERS THROUGH PRAYER

SHELDON D. NEWTON

Intercession is praying for others with a heart of compassion and love. Learn how in this ground-breaking guide on prayer.